POWER TOOLS

for Teaching

POWER TOOLS
for Teaching

BETH LEFGREN

JENNIFER JACKSON

Illustrated by Brent Palmer

BOOKCRAFT
Salt Lake City, Utah

To our families,
who teach us so well

Library of Congress Catalog Card Number: 88-70948

ISBN 0-88494-660-6

5th Printing, 1993

Printed in the United States of America

Contents

Preface

This book was written for you! No matter what teaching situation you find yourself in—home, church, classroom, Scouts, or community—objects are an easy way to clarify ideas and make your lessons more memorable. The purpose of this book is to give you object lessons flexible enough to be personal, yet structured enough to be a lesson's basis.

By using your own creativity, you can use these teaching activities to fit almost any group or situation. You can easily interchange subjects and the objects used to describe them to meet your individual needs.

Subjects are set up alphabetically for easy location and are indexed in the back for your convenience.

As you use object lessons, your ability and creativity in presenting ideas will greatly increase. This will lead to more enthusiasm, and you will become a better teacher. We hope that you find success in using these ideas.

Adversity

Objective: To demonstrate that trials, when properly viewed, can improve us.

Materials Needed: A small piece of coal and a diamond or picture of a diamond.

Procedure: Show the piece of coal. Ask what it is, what it is used for, and how much it might cost. Explain that coal is bought by weight. A ton may include many hundreds of pieces.

Show the diamond (or a picture). Ask what it is, how it is used, and how much it might cost. Explain that diamonds are bought separately and can cost many hundreds of dollars.

Explain that each diamond could have become a piece of coal but instead extreme pressure and heat structured it into a beautiful diamond.

Heavenly Father sends us trials to help us become better individuals. These trials and learning experiences can help us structure ourselves and become more Christlike.

Appearance

Objective: To illustrate how our appearance says much about the type of person we are.

Materials Needed: A can of food with a label on it.

Procedure: Using a labeled can, point out to your group that the label tells us many things about the product. Point out a few of its features: what the item is, nutritional information, calories, and who manufactured it.

Compare this to our own appearance. Explain that our dress, cleanliness, and hair tell others many things about us. Just as a wise consumer checks the labels, so do most people assess our appearance. Jobs, friendships, and many opportunities can be lost or won on the basis of how we present ourselves.

Association

Objective: To depict that the friends with whom we associate and the environment in which we place ourselves can influence the type of person we become.

Materials Needed: A pitcher of water.

Procedure: Ask the group what would happen if you placed the water in the freezer. (It would turn to ice.) Ask what would happen if we left it as it is. (It would eventually become flat and stale.) Ask what would happen if you put it in a pot on the stove and turned the stove on high. (It would begin to boil, and steam would result.)

Liken this to ourselves and the atmosphere we place ourselves in. We can choose friends and activities that will harden us and make us cold, like the ice. We can associate ourselves with people and places that don't change us much one way or another. We stay in a rut and eventually stagnate. Or we can choose a group of people and surroundings that will get us moving and make us want to better ourselves, enabling us to bless the lives of others through our warmth.

Attitude

Objective: To inspire us to have a positive outlook in life.

Materials Needed: A sheet of paper.

Procedure: Start this object lesson by holding up the sheet of paper and telling the group that it represents our lives. We'll have many problems and disappointments in our lives; for example, having a flat tire in the middle of the desert, having to care for a sick relative, missing an airplane or bus, or losing a father or mother. Be specific with these problems. As you name each problem, tear a small piece of paper off. Do this until the entire sheet has been torn into pieces.

Now point out that some people would look at this pile of scraps and say, "Look at this. My whole life has been nothing but problems." Yet others would look at this pile of paper, pick up the paper, and toss it in the air as confetti to celebrate the gift of their lives and the problems they have overcome. If you'd like, you can actually throw the confetti in the air.

Share your desire for them that they might find joy among the trials, for these trials strengthen you and bring blessings.

Scripture Reference: Doctrine and Covenants 121:7 – 8.

Attitude

Objective: To demonstrate that sometimes we allow small difficulties to interfere with seeing great blessings.

Materials Needed: Small pebbles and small pieces of candy.

Procedure: Give each person a pebble and a small piece of candy. Instruct the class members to place the pebbles in their shoes and the candies in their mouths. Tell them to take a short walk. (Although this works best outside, it can be adapted to a classroom situation if needed.)

After the walk, ask the group about their experience. Most will dwell on the discomfort of the pebble and say little about the good taste of the candy.

Explain that sometimes we focus on the small hardships (pebbles) that are part of life and forget the good things (candies) that are all around us.

At this time, discuss the importance of a positive attitude to ourselves and to those around us.

Book of Mormon

Objective: To understand one reason why the Book of Mormon is important to us.

Materials Needed: A map of your state and a map of a city within your state.

Procedure: Explain to the group that you have two maps, one of the state and one of a city. Then ask them which map they would choose if they needed to find a particular street in the city. Explain that the state map is important because it gives us a greater view around the city, as well as showing us where in the state the city is actually located. But to be able to find a specific street, we need the city map because it gives us the detailed information we must have.

Compare the city map to the Book of Mormon. This book was written specifically for us and our needs. It gives us vital gospel information in its fulness. Also point out that the Bible has value to us because it gives an overall account of the history of other of God's children and also provides a good overview or general description of the gospel.

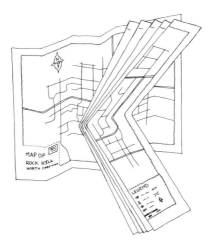

Boundaries

Objective: Boundaries and laws help us become better persons.

Materials Needed: A loaf of bread baked in a bread pan and a loaf of bread baked without a pan.

Preparation: Bake two loaves of bread; one in a regular bread pan, and the other on a cookie sheet.

Procedure: Display the two loaves of bread. Ask what differences the class notices. Be sure to acknowledge that one loaf was baked with a bread pan and one loaf was not.

Explain that we are like the bread dough. We will rise best and become the best shape if we stay within boundaries and obey laws. If we do not, we can spread all over and become misshapen.

Callings in the Church

Objective: To show that maintaining proper perspective can help us to magnify any calling.

Materials Needed: A large, hand-held magnifying glass.

Preparation: You may need to practice this activity beforehand.

Procedure: Use the magnifying glass to view an object from various distances. Discuss what happens when the magnifying glass is held farther away from the object. (The object gets out of focus, inverts, and then decreases in size.)

Explain that, in our callings or positions, we must maintain proper closeness to avoid distortion. We cannot properly magnify any calling if we do not correctly see what we need to do.

Character

Objective: To show that our characters can be enhanced through absorbing correct characteristics.

Materials Needed: Two *fresh* white carnations or white irises, two clear vases, and liquid food coloring.

Preparation: Take one of the vases, and fill it with water and some food coloring. Clip the very end off one of the carnations, and place it into the vase. The carnation will turn the color of the water.

Procedure: Show the white carnation to the class. Discuss its beauty. Explain that our characters are like the carnation: they have a natural and pure beauty.

Clip the end off the undyed carnation and place it into the vase filled with water. Put several drops of food coloring into the water.

Discuss what things can enhance and make a character more beautiful (kindness, patience, modesty, etc.). If desired, extend the discussion to include thoughts on how one or more of these virtues can be achieved.

At this time take out the previously dyed carnation, and show it to the class. You may return to the carnation that was started during class. If it is fresh enough, it will have begun to show signs of the food coloring. Explain that, like the carnation, our inner beauty can be enhanced if it absorbs the right kind of characteristics.

Character

Objective: To show that positive choices can have a permanent effect on a character.

Materials Needed: An immature pumpkin or melon (any smooth-skinned squash or melon will work well) and a pointed object (a stick or sharp pencil).

Preparation: Find a pumpkin patch, and decide on the pumpkin or melon that will best fit your lesson. Have a lesson on making positive choices, and how they will affect your character.

Procedure: Take your class to a field where there is an immature pumpkin. Briefly review the lesson on choices. Show the pumpkin that you previously decided on. Be sure to point out the smooth skin of the pumpkin. Be careful not to step on or damage the pumpkin plant.

Explain that our characters are like the pumpkin, and the choices we make are like the marks we will make on the smooth skin of the pumpkin. Tell the class that it is important that we make our decisions wisely and leave good marks on our characters.

At this point, use the pointed object to mark or write on the pumpkin. Tell the class that the mark will now become part of the pumpkin. Allow the pumpkin to continue its growth.

Bring the fully mature pumpkin to the class so that the mark can be seen. It is effective at this point to again state the lesson objective.

Charity

Objective: To demonstrate how charity can help us to rise to our highest potential as servants of our Heavenly Father.

Materials Needed: Two loaves of homemade bread—one with yeast, one without yeast.

Procedure: Display both loaves of bread. Ask what the class members think made the difference. (Yeast.) Point out that the recipe was followed exactly for both loaves with the exception of one ingredient, the yeast. It's easy to tell which loaf has the yeast.

Explain that in our lives we can have a similar experience. We can develop our character and obey the commandments; but if we omit the important ingredient of charity for all mankind, it will all be for nothing. Without this vital ingredient, we cannot rise to our highest potential.

Scripture Reference: Moroni 7:46—47.

Christ

Objective: To help us gain an understanding that Christ is the only means by which we can return to our Heavenly Father.

Materials Needed: Two small pieces of pvc pipe and a joint that will link them together.

Procedure: Ask the group what our ultimate goal in life should be. (To return to live with our Heavenly Father.) Explain that Christ made it possible for us to return to him through his atonement and resurrection. By believing in him and keeping his commandments, we can return to our Father in Heaven.

Show the two pieces of pvc pipe to the group, and compare these to ourselves and our Heavenly Father. Point out that there is no way that these two pieces will fit together by themselves. Now take the pvc joint and liken that to Christ, who is our mediator. Show how this very special part can bring the other two together. Only through Christ can we receive eternal life.

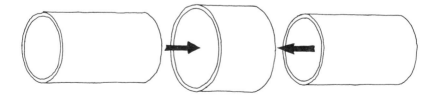

Christ

Objective: To inspire us to commit to follow Christ and his example throughout our lives.

Materials Needed: A compass.

Procedure: As you show the group the compass, explain to them that it is a device for determining directions. It has a needle that always points to the magnetic north pole. A person who is lost can find his way through following an undeviating course with the use of this compass.

Explain that we have a spiritual compass of our own — Jesus Christ. The directions that we receive from him constantly point us toward our Heavenly Father. Though we may be lost, by casting our eyes upon him and following his undeviating course, we will most certainly find ourselves being welcomed back to our heavenly home.

Christ

Objective: To inspire us to develop a closer relationship with the Savior.

Materials Needed: A glass of water, an index card, a penny, and tape.

Procedure: Briefly have a discussion with the group about the traps that Satan has set for us. Explain that Christ can protect us from those traps if we stay close to him.

Display the glass of water. Explain that it represents the traps Satan has waiting for us. Then place the index card on top of the glass of water. State that this illustrates how Christ can protect us from the traps. Next put the penny on top of the index card, likening ourselves to it. Quickly pull the card across the glass: the penny will plop into the water.

Ask why the penny fell into the water. (It was merely resting on top of the card. It was not securely attached.) Ask the class if their relationship with the Savior is so strong and close that no hardship, trial, or temptation could separate them. Ask them how we can more closely bind ourselves to the Savior. Help them bring out that learning more of Christ and his mission and obeying that which he has taught us through his example are both means by which we can get closer to him.

Tape the penny to the index card. Explain that the tape represents those things that will bind us to Christ. Follow this up by doing the experiment again. Challenge the group to develop their relationship with the Savior so that he might protect them from the many traps that Satan has set.

Communication

Objective: To demonstrate that verbal skills, by themselves, are not always enough for good communication.

Materials Needed: Portable writing surfaces, blank paper, copies of a simple design (several geometric figures combined together are excellent), and pencils.

Procedure: Pair off the members of the group. Determine which member of each pair will describe and which one will listen. Have each pair sit back to back. Explain that the describer must use verbal clues only to help the listener draw the design given. Give the listener a writing surface, a blank paper, and a pencil. Give the describer a copy of the design. Proceed with the activity as described. Have a time limit.

Make observations as to the results of this experiment. Help the group realize that if visual communications had been used in addition to the verbal, the results would have been much improved.

Cooperation

Objective: To show that difficult things can be accomplished when we stand together.

Materials Needed: About twenty-five to thirty wooden matches and a rubber band.

Procedure: Take one of the wooden matches, and try to stand it up. Express that it is difficult to do. Now take the remaining matches, and gather them together in one group. Wrap them with the rubber band to secure them together.

Explain that we are like the matches. When we stand and work together, we can accomplish many things that are difficult.

Cooperation

Objective: To show that solutions are found easiest through cooperation.

Materials Needed: A large picture or a scripture printed on a large sheet of paper.

Preparation: Cut the picture or scripture into several pieces (like a puzzle).

Procedure: Give every class member at least one piece of the puzzle. Ask if anyone can tell you what the picture (scripture) is. Inquire as to why no one can identify the picture.

Explain that with some problems, we can only see parts of the picture. This can make it difficult to come up with a solution.

At this point, have everyone work on the puzzle together. When the puzzle is solved, discuss how easily the puzzle was solved once cooperation was used.

Cooperation

Objective: To illustrate that effective cooperation takes working together.

Materials Needed: Two lengths of rope for every three persons.

Procedure: Separate the class into groups of three. Assign one person in each group to be the leader. Place the leader between his two partners, and tie the leader's right leg to one companion's left leg. Tie the leader's left leg to the other companion's right leg. Now ask the groups to walk.

Explain to the groups that we work with and depend upon other people all of our lives. To work effectively, we must learn to communicate and coordinate our efforts.

Divine Nature

Objective: To show that all of us have seeds of our divine nature.

Materials Needed: One apple and a knife.

Procedure: Cut the apple in half widthwise, and show the inner part. Tell the class that every apple has a similar five-sided star inside that holds seeds. No matter what the condition of the apple is (withered, bruised, or ready for picking), the star and its seeds are still inside.

Explain that we are like the apple. Each of us has the potential (seed) of becoming like Heavenly Father. No matter what happens to us, we still have the seeds of a divine nature and the potential of godhood.

Eternal Progression

Objective: To give a visual demonstration of the concepts of premortality, death, and resurrection.

Materials Needed: One glove.

Procedure: Show your ungloved hand. Label or call the hand "spirit." Explain that when we lived in the premortal life with Heavenly Father, we were spirits. We could move (demonstrate physically with your hand) and think and spiritually grow.

Explain that we knew we could not be complete until we had gained a body, and so we chose to be born into mortality. At this point put the glove on the hand labeled or called "spirit." Explain that our body could still move and think and grow in many ways. It knew pain and joy.

Then the body died. Take off the glove, and lay it down on a table or your lap. Explain that the body no longer moved but that the spirit was still alive. It still moved and thought and could even grow spiritually.

When we are resurrected, our spirit will be reunited with our body. Place the glove back on the hand. State that this time Heavenly Father will give it a special glory, and the body and the spirit will never be separated again.

Faith

Objective: To gain an understanding of the true meaning of faith.

Materials Needed: Paper and a small treat or reward.

Preparation: This lesson involves a treasure hunt. Before the lesson, prepare and hide several papers with clues on them. These clues should lead the class members from one place to the next, finally ending with finding the reward.

Procedure: Begin your lesson by telling the group that somewhere you have hidden a special reward for them. Hand them the first clue, and tell them that following the clues will lead them to their reward.

After they have completed the treasure hunt and found their reward, sit down and have a short discussion with them. Ask them why they knew there was a reward at the end of the treasure hunt. (They believed what you told them.) Ask: If you believed there was a reward but didn't follow the clues or directions, would you have gotten the reward? (No.) Bring out that the class members' beliefs plus their actions helped them receive their reward.

Explain that faith uses this same principle. Heavenly Father has told us that there is a wonderful reward waiting for us. If we believe him but don't follow the instructions he has given us, we'll never find that reward. If we take action and strictly follow the directions, we will receive the reward. Belief plus action equals faith.

Faith

Objective: To illustrate how faith can give us courage and strength in our daily lives.

Materials Needed: A potted plant, foil, and crushed chocolate wafers.

Preparation: Cover the soil of a potted plant with foil. (You may need to remove some dirt to allow for enough top space.) Finely crush several chocolate wafers, and spread them on top of the foil. It will look like potting soil.

Procedure: Begin your lesson by displaying the potted plant and telling class members that the soil around the plant is good and if they eat it they'll really like it. Take out a spoon, and ask who has enough faith in you to eat some of the soil. Sometimes this takes some coaxing.

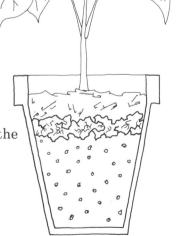

After an individual has tasted the soil and realized what it really is, explain that his faith gave him the courage and strength to do what was asked. Liken this to our faith in any area, such as faith in the healing power of the priesthood, faith in what the prophet instructs us to do, or faith in Christ.

Flag

Objective: To show that the flag is more than just several pieces of material.

Materials Needed: One flag of the United States, one piece of red material, one piece of white material, and one piece of blue material.

Procedure: Hold up the blue material. Ask what could be done with it. (Make a pillow, use for a rag, etc.) Do the same with the red and the white material also. After this, hold up the flag. Be sure to use the proper respect in handling it.

Explain that even though the flag is made of ordinary red, white, and blue material, it should be treated with respect. Discuss why it deserves respect. Be sure to point out that it represents more than just a nation—it represents many people and their hopes for the future.

Free Agency

Objective: To help the group understand that each choice we make helps to determine our future.

Materials Needed: Magnetic alphabet letters and a metal board.

Procedure: Explain that with a full set of the letters of the alphabet we can create any word we want. First we determine the word we want to write, and then we choose the appropriate letters that will spell it. Give a couple of examples on your board. Explain that we can even begin to put the words together and write a book.

Explain that, in a sense, each of us is writing a book. The book is our future. Instead of using letters and words, the book is compiled of the choices we make. Free agency gives us the opportunity to be the author of our own book. No one else will write it for us. The outcome of this book will determine our ultimate destination. To make this book a success, we must first decide how we want it to end and then make the appropriate choices that will lead us to that conclusion (just as we first decide which word we want to spell and then select the proper letters).

Explain that, if we choose the appropriate letters, our books will be successful. Then put together the letters on the board to spell *godhood.*

Variations: This activity can also easily be done with chalk and a chalkboard.

Scripture Reference: 2 Nephi 10:23.

Free Agency

Objective: To demonstrate the effects free agency can have on our lives.

Materials Needed: Paper and a few various props.

Preparation: Read over the following activity, and prepare the paths, cards, and props that it calls for.

Procedure: This activity works best in a large room or outside. Prepare for the activity by first cutting out paper stepping-stones. You should have enough steps to make two paths. Position these paths so that they start in the same place but gradually veer off in different directions. One path represents choices we make that lead us closer to Heavenly Father, and the other represents choices that take us further away.

Next, make the game cards the class members will pick. There should be two sets of cards, one for each path. The game cards represent the choices we make in our lives. The first cards might read: "I left the spirit world today and received my mortal body. Take 3 steps." "I grew and learned many good things from my parents. Take 1 step." "I turned eight years old and was able to be baptized. Take 3 steps." At this point, the paths should begin to separate, and the cards should first lead the class members on the path away from Heavenly Father. Make a few cards that illustrate choices a young child would make, such as "Watched TV instead of doing homework" or "Teasing sister in sacrament meeting." Gradually the choices displayed should become more serious.

Take the class members through the teenage years, touching on appropriate areas of temptations. This should lead into adulthood. Show some side effects from the decisions made earlier. This could include "Due to unworthiness, could not be married in the temple" or "Health problems resulting from disobedience to Word of Wisdom." Depict an unhappy life. As individuals travel down this path, place yourself and the rest of the group farther away to project a feeling of isolation. The end of the path should leave the individuals totally alone, with as bland surroundings as possible. This will give them an empty, void feeling.

Contrast this by immediately following the correct path. The choices on these cards should show the desire to do right even when otherwise tempted. Try to produce a feeling of happiness. Appropriate props can be used: if the class members graduate from college, a cap and diploma could be given. As individuals draw nearer to the end of this path, other group members should be waiting for them. Decorations and fun refreshments can be waiting to show the celebration that will take place on their arrival. A large picture of the Savior would also add to this scene. All of this will help to develop the anxious, glad feeling you want to achieve.

You can modify this basic activity to fit your group or needs. It takes quite a bit of preparation, but the effects of it will leave lasting impressions on those involved. Without anyone telling them, they will better understand the importance of using their free agency wisely.

Goals

Objective: To point out the importance of planning small, consecutive goals in order to achieve a long-range goal.

Materials Needed: Dominoes.

Procedure: Line up three rows of dominoes, the first with a small gap in the middle so that the whole row will not fall down. The second row should have a domino off center to keep a chain reaction from occurring. The third row should be straight with all the dominoes close enough to ensure the successive fall of all of them.

Start the lesson with a brief discussion about planning goals. Explain that in order to achieve a long-range goal, we must have several small, well-planned goals to keep on course to our ultimate goals. Knock down the row of dominoes with the gap in the middle. Point out that if we skip a vital step in our progressive goals, we will not succeed.

Knock down the second row with the off-centered domino. Use this to point out that if we don't stay on course with our goals, we will not achieve our desired results.

To illustrate success through strictly followed, well-planned goals, knock down the third row, which will completely fall down. This lesson becomes more meaningful if you give an example of a long-range goal and actually plan out the key steps that will help you achieve it.

Goals

Objective: To demonstrate the value of setting goals.

Materials Needed: A candy bar and a tray full of a variety of small objects.

Procedure: Display the tray full of objects. Ask one member of the group to choose an item. Tell him if he chooses the correct object, he will get a reward (the candy bar). After he chooses, tell him it was not the right item, and then ask if he would like some clues. Give him two or three clues that will allow him to single out the item you have in mind. After he chooses the right object, give him the candy bar.

Explain to the group that there are many wonderful rewards awaiting each of us. However, the random selection of miscellaneous activities or studies will not get us any closer to our rewards. We must set goals with specific steps that will enable us to have a clear picture of what we need to achieve. If we follow through with this type of planning, we will find what we are seeking.

Goals

Objective: To show that it is more effective to set and accomplish goals individually than to set goals in large amounts.

Materials Needed: Seven coins.

Procedure: Tell the group that you have seven coins. Ask one person to catch the coins when you throw them. Tell him to catch as many as he can. Take the coins and toss them all at once to the catcher. Ask how many were caught. Pick up the coins, and toss them one at a time. Ask how many coins were caught this time.

Explain that the coins are like goals. When we try to plan many goals at one time, some may not be accomplished (caught). The same amount of goals can be planned and more will be accomplished if they are worked on one or two at a time.

Gossip

Objective: To show that the effects of gossip, carelessly released, are gathered back only with great difficulty.

Materials Needed: Down feathers (any light, easily blown object will do), wind, and a paper sack.

Procedure: Have the class sit in an open area outside. Place the feathers into the paper sack, and give it to one student. Allow that student to open the bag and let the feathers drop in an open area. Personally instruct the feathers not to go any farther. Have the student sit with the class again.

Briefly discuss how the feathers are like gossip. They are easily turned loose and allowed to go where they will, even though specifically instructed to stay where they were released. Tell the student or class to go collect all the feathers. After they return, ask if it was easy to find the feathers again.

Explain that the effects of gossip are easily released but difficult to gather back.

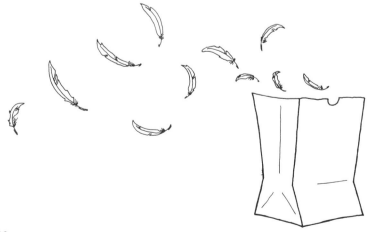

Habits

Objective: To show that habits can affect our ability to withstand temptation.

Materials Needed: Several pieces of rope for each volunteer.

Procedure: Ask one class member to sit on a chair, and ask another class member to stand in front of a chair. Take a piece of rope, and tie the seated class member's legs together (not to the chair). Repeat the same operation with the standing class member. Ask the seated person to stand up and the standing person to sit down. Both class members should be able to do this. After they resume their initial position, use the additional ropes to tie them more securely (do not tie them to the chairs).

Explain that the ropes are like habits. When we reinforce our habits, it becomes harder for us to move to a different position or character.

This lesson can be expanded upon by using the idea of good habits (standing) and bad habits (sitting). It is easier for the standing person to fall into a sitting position (good to bad) than for a sitting person to stand (bad to good).

Habits

Objective: To inspire group members to develop good habits.

Materials Needed: Several washcloths.

Procedure: Have several unfolded washcloths in a pile. Explain that the washcloths fit best in your cabinet if folded in thirds. Begin to fold the washcloths as you speak. Point out that at first it wasn't easy to fold them in thirds. Your mother never did it that way, and previously you had always folded them in quarters. As you began folding them this new way, it took concentration and self-discipline. Gradually it became easier and easier. Now you can fold those washcloths in thirds without thinking about it. It has become a habit, or a routine. You should have a stack of folded washcloths at this point.

Compare this to developing any good habit. At first it is much harder. It takes more time, and you can get discouraged. However, if you stick to it, it will gradually become easier and easier until it is a habit or routine. Challenge each of the class members to develop one good habit.

Habits

Objective: Habits are harder to break the more they are used.

Materials Needed: Sewing thread and two sticks.

Procedure: Have one individual (or two individuals) hold the two sticks about six to twelve inches apart. Wind the thread around the two sticks once and tie. Ask the stick holder to break the thread. Wind the string around the stick three times. Ask the stick holder to break the string. Add layers of string, and repeat the process until the string does not break. Ask the stick holder the difference between the first and last time.

Explain that habits, both good and bad, are like the string. Habits can be easily broken when new but are difficult to get rid of after repeated use.

This demonstration can be focused on either good or bad habits. Explain that bad habits should be broken early or that good habits should be encouraged and strengthened through use.

Holy Ghost

Objective: To help the group understand that the Holy Ghost helps protect us and can surround us with peace.

Materials Needed: A large, soft quilt.

Procedure: Wrap yourself in the quilt, and refer to it as a comforter. Explain that people call it a comforter because it is soft and warm and can make us feel very comfortable.

State that *Comforter* is also another name for the Holy Ghost. Ask why the Holy Ghost would be called a comforter, or indicate that the Holy Ghost can help us feel comfortable when we listen to his promptings and allow his influence to surround our lives.

Scripture Reference: John 14:26–27.

Additional Idea: Both comforters can also include others in their reach.

Individuality

Objective: To show that each of us is an individual, even though we came from the same parent (Heavenly Father).

Materials Needed: A small tree with large leaves, paper, and crayons.

Procedure: Instruct the students to pick one leaf off the tree. Have each student cover his leaf with a piece of paper and color lightly to produce a pattern (leaf rubbing). Compare the leaf rubbings and notice the differences and similarities.

Explain that we are like the leaves. We are similar in some ways, but we are all individuals and different in some way, even though we might come from the same parents.

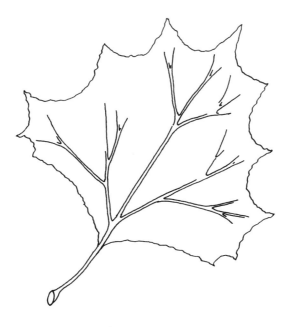

Journals

Objective: To illustrate the purpose and value of keeping a journal.

Materials Needed: A large cardboard box and several of your favorite possessions, such as a trophy, record album, sweater, pictures, cleats, or basketball.

Procedure: Tell your group that these are some of your favorite possessions. Try to pick them all up, and briefly tell the class what each item is. Explain how difficult it is to hold all the items at once. Also point out how easily you could drop one of the items and lose it, as well as damage any of them. Take the cardboard box, and carefully place each item in it. This box will help to keep the items from being broken or lost.

Use this demonstration to point out the purpose of journals. They help us to keep our very favorite memories and experiences from being lost and keep all the details intact.

Judgment

Objective: To show that outward appearances are not always what they seem.

Materials Needed: Sugar cookies, regular icing, and salted icing.

Preparation: Prepare a small batch of icing, using seven to eight times more salt than called for. Ice several cookies with this icing, and decorate them as you would regular cookies. These cookies could also have their dough salted. Ice and decorate the rest of the cookies with regular icing. Be sure you have enough cookies for the entire class.

Procedure: Show the plate of cookies to the class. Have the exact amount of cookies needed (be sure to include the salted cookies). Pass the cookies around as you would a treat. Protests will soon be registered.

Explain that people are like the cookies. Outward appearances are not always accurate in judging people or their actions. Be sure to have a regular sugar cookie to replace each salted one.

This lesson can use a beautifully decorated styrofoam cake instead of cookies.

Judgment

Objective: To show that sight judgments are not always accurate.

Materials Needed: Two pans—one spotless on the inside and dirty on the outside, the other dirty on the inside and shiny on the outside.

Procedure: Show the two pans, being careful not to expose the inside. Ask the class members which one they would like to have their food cooked in tonight. Discuss how the choice was made, and then show the inside of the chosen pan.

Explain that people are like the pans. Persons are not always the way they seem on the outside. We should not make decisions based on looks or first impressions.

Judgment

Objective: To motivate the group to have a desire to look for the good in others.

Materials Needed: A watermelon.

Procedure: Let the group see the melon. Point out that it's hard, plain, and maybe even a little scuffed up on the outside. Its outward appearance doesn't give a hint as to the treat that is inside.

Split the melon, and show the red, juicy fruit. Make the observation that the seeds in it can make it annoying to eat the fruit, but it is a simple matter to pick them out and set them aside.

As the group is eating the melon, draw a parallel between the watermelon and people. Many don't dress, act, or appear as we do; but if we are willing to look beyond surface appearances, it will be worth our effort. We can find qualities of humor, kindness, intellect, and much more. Sometimes we'll still find a few annoying habits, just like the seeds, but it is a simple matter to overlook them. Then we can truly enjoy the most important part of a person.

Judgment

Objective: To discourage individuals from judging others.

Materials Needed: A one-dollar bill and one hundred pennies.

Procedure: Display both the pennies and the dollar bill. Examine some of their differences. The pennies are hard, while the dollar bill is flexible. The pennies tend to make more noise than the dollar bill. Each is a different color. The pennies are also heavier than the dollar bill. Though there are many differences in the items, both have the same worth and value.

Compare this to people. Many are hard to get along with, while others are more flexible. Some individuals are talkative; others are shy. There are different colors and nationalities. There are also weight differences. Just as the money differed in many ways, so do people. Yet all people have the same worth and value.

Leadership

Objective: To show that the kind of leadership we give is very important.

Materials Needed: Twelve flat toothpicks, string, and a rubber band.

Procedure: Take the toothpicks, and gather them together in a bunch. Do not tie them. Discuss what could be done to help the toothpicks stand up.

Explain that the toothpicks are like a group that needs leadership. This leadership can be offered in three ways:

1. The careless leader. Tie four toothpicks together very loosely, and try to stand them up. Explain that this leader does not use follow-up and encouragement. Consequently, this leader's group will fall down on the projects.

2. The strict leader. Tie four toothpicks together very tightly. Tie them tightly enough so that the toothpicks crack or break. Explain that this leader uses pressure, occasionally criticism, or sarcasm to insure success as a leader.

3. The flexible leader. Wrap four toothpicks with a rubber band. Explain that this type of leader encourages and follows through on assignments but never binds tightly. There is a lot of give and take, and this leader will consider the needs of his group.

Leadership

Objective: To point out the importance of following Christ's footsteps in regards to his perfect example of leadership.

Materials Needed: A pattern to trace around, chalk, and a chalkboard.

Procedure: Begin this lesson by inviting a class member to come up and draw a picture of whatever shape or design your pattern is. Do not show them the pattern but give a brief description of it.

After they have done this, bring out your pattern, and have them carefully trace around it. Compare how different the two drawings are.

Use this to illustrate that if we are to be the type of leaders that the Lord expects us to be, we must follow the perfect example or pattern he gave us through his life. This cannot be done with random attempts. We must learn of him and his ways through much study and prayer.

Brainstorm about several of his leadership characteristics, for example: guidance from Heavenly Father through prayer, humility, long-suffering, forgiveness, and so forth.

Leadership

Objective: To help the class members understand that one must have a clear vision to help another.

Materials Needed: Toothpaste, two pairs of eyeglasses, paper, and a pencil.

Procedure: Use two people with eyeglasses, or provide two pairs of clear, nonprescription glasses for use. Liberally smear the lenses of one pair of glasses with toothpaste. Give the glasses to the first volunteer. Place a small dot of toothpaste on the other pair (be sure that there is a big enough dot to restrict vision slightly). Give them to the second volunteer.

Have the second volunteer begin to draw a picture of a person, an object, or a design. Ask if it is easy to draw. Have the first volunteer help finish the picture. The result will speak for itself.

Explain that we cannot help someone overcome a failing unless we are free from that problem ourselves.

Scripture Reference: Matthew 7:3–5.

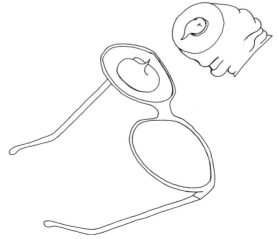

Leadership

Objective: To show that being a good leader requires a certain amount of knowledge and insight.

Materials Needed: Two bowls of pudding, two spoons, two waterproof coverings, and two blindfolds.

Procedure: Place two volunteers directly across from each other, and give each a bowl of pudding, a spoon, and a waterproof covering. Then blindfold each. Instruct the volunteers that they are responsible for feeding their partner the bowl of pudding. Proceed with the activity.

After the volunteers have cleaned up, explain that being a leader requires knowledge and an ability to learn. Also point out that we must be careful whom we choose to follow. Merely acting without a clear vision of what we want to accomplish results in confusion and inefficient results.

Marriage

Objective: To encourage us to constantly strive to enrich our marriages.

Materials Needed: Two packages of powdered punch mix, sugar, and water.

Procedure: Mix both packages of punch, one according to the directions and the other without the sugar. First, serve the punch without sugar. The group will observe how bitter and sour it tastes. Next serve the punch that has been mixed properly.

While the students drink the punch, liken the punch without the sugar to a marriage in which both partners are not completely following the directions that the Lord has given us for marriage. If we do not do all we can to make our marriage a happy one, it can be a very bitter experience. However, if we follow the directions and add that little bit of sugar, the marriage will be pleasing and satisfying to us.

If the situation does not permit serving punch, this lesson can be given as a very effective verbal example.

Missionary Work

Objective: To understand that the gospel must be shared to be enjoyed.

Materials Needed: An orange.

Procedure: Tell everyone how good it will be to eat the orange. While peeling the orange, comment on how good it smells and how juicy it is. After the orange is peeled, take some time to admire it. Remove one segment, and begin eating it. Express how good it tastes: not too sour, very juicy, and so on. Ask someone to tell how good it tastes. (He or she won't know.) Then ask why that person doesn't know. (Because he or she has not tasted it.)

Explain that the gospel is like the orange. Everyone can see that you are enjoying it, but until you offer to share it, no one will know for himself. Share the orange with the class members.

Music

Objective: To show that music can be used for good or bad.

Materials Needed: One match.

Procedure: Strike the match, and let it burn for a brief time. Extinguish the flame, and properly dispose of the match. Discuss how fire can be valuable when used properly and how it can cause destruction if misused.

Explain that music is like fire. It can raise our sights to help us become better people, or it can debase and destroy us.

Obedience

Objective: To illustrate that obedience to the covenants we make with the Lord will draw us closer to him.

Materials Needed: Two individual binder rings, a large picture of Christ glued to poster board, three sheets of colored cellophane, and one clear sheet of cellophane. (Most florists have the cellophane.)

Procedure: Prepare the visual aid by punching two holes in the top of the poster board and in corresponding places on each piece of cellophane. Layer the cellophane on top of the poster, with the clear piece directly against the picture. Attach the cellophane and poster together with the rings. Place this on an easel for the class.

Introduce the topic of obedience to the covenants we make with the Lord. Discuss the different areas of covenants: baptism, endowment, and sealing. Explain that if we are faithful to our baptismal covenants, we will draw closer to the Savior and the veil that separates us will be thinned. Pull back the first sheet of cellophane. The picture of Christ will look a little clearer. Repeat the process for the next two areas. All that will cover the picture at this point is the clear cellophane. Use this to illustrate how thin the veil can become and how close we can draw to the Savior through obedience.

Scripture Reference: Doctrine and Covenants 88:63.

Obedience

Objective: To show that only complete obedience will allow for complete effectiveness.

Materials Needed: Sap from a pine tree, margarine, soap, and water.

Preparation: Make an instruction card with the following information: (1) grease hands liberally with butter, margarine, or solid shortening; (2) wash with soap and water.

Procedure: Ask for a volunteer. Have the volunteer put some sap on his hands. (Do not let the volunteer get it on his clothing.) Give the volunteer the information card, and tell him to use only the second group of directions.

While the volunteer is trying to wash the sap off, explain how important it is to follow all directions. Discuss what could happen when directions are not followed completely (leaving ingredients out of food, not allowing bread to rise, skipping steps when making models, etc.).

When the volunteer comes back, he will still have the sap on his hands. Now give the volunteer some butter, and have him completely follow *all* directions. The sap will come off completely.

Parenting

Objective: To stress the importance of rules and guidelines for raising children.

Materials Needed: A bouquet of freshly cut flowers and a bouquet of weeds.

Procedure: Tell the group that many in society have adopted the view that we put too many restrictions on children nowadays. These people believe that rather than indoctrinate children with our own beliefs, we should let them decide for themselves.

Ask the class to apply this same principle to a flower garden. The garden is not watered, weeded, or pruned. And seeds are not planted in it. It is simply left on its own. Ask the class what they suppose the flower garden will produce. Display the bouquet of weeds.

Contrast this by describing a flower garden that has been carefully pruned, weeded, and watered. Seeds were selected and planted with the utmost consideration. Ask the class what they suppose this flower garden would produce. Display the bouquet of freshly cut flowers.

Liken this to raising children and the guidance, direction, and care we must use to raise them.

Scripture Reference:
Proverbs 22:6.

Peace

Objective: To encourage harmony at home.

Materials Needed: A pot, a large serving spoon, a delicate goblet or glass, and a small teaspoon.

Procedure: Begin by taking the large spoon and banging the kettle loudly several times. Then take the teaspoon, and carefully tap the glass, producing a delicate ringing sound.

Point out to the group that nagging, criticizing, shouting, and name-calling are much the same as banging the pot. It hurts our ears, and causes us to want to avoid the sound as much as possible.

In contrast, the tinkling sound of the glass can be compared to cheerfulness, encouragement, and displays of love. Those pleasant sounds are appealing and make the listener yearn for more. Explain to the group that through controlling our voice and attitude we can make our home a haven where family members desire to be.

Perseverance

Objective: To understand what perseverance is and why it is important.

Materials Needed: Individually wrapped pieces of taffy and gum (enough for your group).

Procedure: Give everyone in your group a piece of taffy, and let the class members begin eating it. While they eat the taffy, explain that many times something is expected of us, whether it be a task, an assignment, or simply a commitment to be true to the standards we have set for ourselves. We generally start out with a good effort. But after a while, pressures, problems, and obstacles find their way to us, and our efforts begin to dissolve—almost like the taffy that was just eaten.

Hand out the gum to group members. As they chew it, explain that we can prove that we are made of tougher ingredients if we will persevere, even though the times are rough and the pressures and temptations come time after time. Liken the quality of perseverance to the gum they are chewing. No matter how many times they apply pressure and chew, the gum still remains. Close by telling them that the Lord has promised great things to those who persevere and endure to the end.

Scripture Reference: Doctrine and Covenants 121:8.

Perseverance

Objective: To show that size is not important when persevering.

Materials Needed: A previously mailed letter with a postage stamp on it.

Procedure: Hold up the letter, and ask the class where this letter might have come from and what it went through to get to your house (canceled, sorted, bagged). Discuss what helped the letter to arrive (postage clerks, planes, etc.). Point out that even though the postage stamp is small, the letter would not have arrived without it. Express appreciation that the stamp stuck to the letter so that it would arrive at your house.

Explain that we can be like the postage stamp and stick to our responsibilities. Remind the class that size or outward importance is not necessary to finish a task and feel accomplishment.

Potential

Objective: To inspire class members to strive a little harder to achieve their highest potential.

Materials Needed: A rope (the longer, the better).

Procedure: Coil a rope, and place it beside you. Begin by asking group members how far they think the rope could be stretched. Ask them if it could reach halfway across the room or perhaps even out of the room. Select an individual to take one end of the rope and stretch it out.

Liken the rope to us. We have an abundance of potential that's coiled up within us. The only way to tell how far that potential can take us is by uncoiling it and actively seeing what we can accomplish. How sad it would be to look back on our lives when we're seventy or eighty and say, "I wonder how far I could have gone if I'd really tried?"

Prayer

Objective: To show that prayer must have the correct connections to work effectively.

Materials Needed: A telephone.

Procedure: Show the telephone, and have class members discuss its use and functions. Ask questions about its power source, distance use, correct connections, and parts (i.e., mouthpiece and earpiece). Be sure to bring out the necessity for having a working phone on both sides of any conversation. After the discussion, ask if the telephone would be effective with only one part or side working.

Compare the telephone to prayer. Explain that prayer, to be effective, must have all its parts in working order. Stress the importance of listening as well as speaking. Remind the class that the Holy Ghost is the power source, and, unlike the telephone, prayer is available anytime and anywhere.

Priesthood Power

Objective: To understand that the priesthood must have the correct keys to function correctly.

Materials Needed: Car keys.

Procedure: Tell the class to imagine that there is a new car in the parking lot that they can use. Describe the details of the car (horsepower, rate of acceleration, body design, engine size, etc.). State that no matter how powerful the car is, it is still dependent upon the proper keys.

Explain that priesthood power must also come through the proper authority (keys) in order to function correctly.

Discussion of priesthood authority and its functions is appropriate here.

Priesthood Power

Objective: To show that priesthood readiness depends upon spiritual strength.

Materials Needed: Two flashlights—one with weak batteries, one with strong batteries.

Procedure: Display the two flashlights, and turn them on. Let the class discover the differences between the two flashlights and why they are different. Be sure the discussion includes the differences in the power sources (weak versus strong battery). Ask which flashlight would be the most useful in a time of need.

Explain that the flashlight is like the priesthood and that the power source is our spirituality. Discuss what things can weaken our spiritual power source. (Profanity, pornography, violence, rebelliousness, etc.) Express how important it would be to have functioning priesthood light and power during a time of need.

Additional Idea: Point out that when priesthood power is low, it can be placed within a power source for recharging. Lead the discussion as to what these power sources could be. (Church attendance, scripture reading, paying tithes, proper language, etc.)

Priesthood Power

Objective: To gain an understanding of how priesthood blessings can help us.

Materials Needed: A heavy object and a lever and fulcrum.

Procedure: Display a heavy object, and explain that you can't lift it alone. You need something to aid you in this process. Set up the fulcrum and lever, sliding the lever under the heavy object. Demonstrate how it works, and point out that this made your load seem much lighter and easier to handle. It enabled you to complete the task.

Explain that there are times in our lives when we feel that the burden we have been given is too heavy to lift. The Lord has given us a way to receive assistance. Liken the fulcrum and lever to the priesthood and blessings. A blessing can help us deal with those things that are too heavy. It will not necessarily take the burden away, but it will provide a means by which we can complete what is required of us.

Priorities

Objective: To point out that we can accomplish more and feel better about ourselves if we set priorities to work on in our lives.

Materials Needed: A small desk drawer cluttered with various items.

Procedure: Display the cluttered desk drawer. Explain that sometimes we feel like that cluttered desk drawer. We stuff so many things into our lives that we even forget what we're supposed to be doing and often feel out of control.

Begin to sort out the drawer. Toss out items that are useless, and neatly put in order the remaining objects. While you are doing this, tell the group that we must regularly evaluate our lives and toss out those things that are taking up space and are not useful. Then we must take stock of the priorities we have left and put them in order. If we will do this, we will feel better about ourselves, and our best efforts will be given to those things that matter the most.

Scripture Reference: Doctrine and Covenants 88:119.

Priorities

Objective: To show that temporal activities will fill in after spiritual priorities are established.

Materials Needed: A large glass bottle filled with sand and another large bottle filled with medium-sized rocks.

Procedure: Prepare for this object lesson by defining temporal activities and spiritual priorities. Indicate that the sand represents temporal priorities (housecleaning, yard work, novels, movies, etc.) and that the rocks represent spiritual priorities (temple work, home teaching, family prayer, scriptures, home evening, etc.).

Explain that the prophets have counseled us to use spiritual priorities to help us become better people. Discuss how hard it can be to fit spiritual priorities into our lives.

Take the bottle of sand, and place it where it is easily seen. Take one of the rocks, and give it a label (for instance, home teaching). Push it down into the sand. Express how easy it was. Repeat the procedure several times. After using several rocks, you will find it harder to fit the rocks into the sand. Express this in terms of fitting spiritual priorities into temporal activities.

Take the rocks out of the sand, and place them with the other rocks in the glass jar. Explain that we can accomplish more by using the spiritual priorities as a basis and fitting temporal activities around them. At this point, pour the bottle of sand into the bottle of rocks.

Priorities

Objective: To show the value of concentrating our efforts on the basic priorities in our lives.

Materials Needed: A large red apple and a small red apple.

Procedure: Begin this lesson by explaining to your group that when an apple tree is loaded with apples in the early summer, the experienced farmer thins his tree and discards a portion of the apples. This keeps the tree limbs from splitting under their heavy burden and enables the tree to provide nutrition to the remaining apples, allowing them to develop into large, juicy apples.

Display the small apple. Explain that at times we get busy with too many things and spread ourselves too thin. Then the results are like that of the split limbs and the small apples.

Sometimes it becomes necessary to thin out the things in our lives. By concentrating our efforts on the priorities we have set, we can have results like the large apple. Display the large apple. Express your hope that the things in the class members' lives that matter most will produce good fruit.

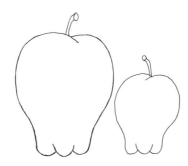

Procrastination

Objective: To inspire us to do what is required quickly, without hesitation.

Materials Needed: Hot and cold tap water, two bowls, food coloring, and an eyedropper.

Procedure: Begin the lesson by conducting an experiment. Fill one bowl with very hot tap water and the other bowl with very cold tap water. Wait until the water has quit moving. Then quickly add three drops of food coloring into each bowl. Point out that the food coloring spreads rapidly in the hot water and much slower in the cold water.

Use this demonstration in a discussion about procrastinating what must be done. If we dread, put off, and complain about our job, we're like the cold water. The job can become a long and agonizing process. If we quickly dig in with a positive attitude, the task can be done quickly, allowing us to move on to other things.

Pure Thought

Objective: To illustrate that contact with pornography or profanity leaves residual effects.

Materials Needed: One ripe orange and one onion.

Preparation: Slice the orange and onion. Layer them together in a closed container for about one hour. Remove the onion and discard it. Arrange the orange attractively on a plate for the lesson.

Procedure: Show what a delicious looking orange you have brought for the lesson. Tell the class that you are anxious to let everyone taste it. Pass the orange slices around. Ask for comments on the taste of the orange.

Explain that the orange had only a brief encounter with an onion and is no longer associated with it. Liken the orange to us before true repentance and the onion to profanity and pornography. Explain that allowing corrupt ideas to enter our lives, even briefly, can leave lasting effects. Further explain, however, that complete and true repentance can restore our pure minds and thoughts to the point that we can be found worthy to eventually enter our Father's presence again.

Pure Thought

Objective: To realize the importance of avoiding profanity and pornography.

Materials Needed: Some masking tape and dark felt.

Procedure: Explain that the Lord has instructed us to keep our thoughts pure. To do this, it is necessary to avoid all pornography and profanity. When we expose our minds to this type of thing, it clutters our thoughts with things degrading and impure.

Illustrate this point by wrapping masking tape around your hand sticky side out and blotting the tape to a dark piece of felt. Have the class observe what happens to the tape. Fuzz from the felt should cover it.

Explain that our minds are similar to the tape. When exposed to inappropriate materials, our minds retain those things. Our thoughts become crowded with things that are unholy and impure. Once the thoughts are implanted, they are nearly impossible to remove. Invite a member to try and remove pieces of the fuzz from the tape.

Scripture Reference: Doctrine and Covenants 121:45.

Pure Thought

Objective: To show that a clean mind is the product of the ideas put in.

Materials Needed: An empty paper towel roll, clean white paper, and dirty paper (newspaper is good).

Preparation: Crumple the white paper and dirty paper into balls.

Procedure: Show that the paper towel roll is empty on the inside. Push the dirty paper balls into the paper towel roll. Continue until they begin to come out the other end.

Explain that this paper towel roll is like our minds. When we read and think filthy ideas, unclean ideas and words will clutter our minds and eventually be expressed verbally.

Begin to push the clean paper into the paper towel roll. Explain that when we fill our minds with clean and uplifting material, it will eventually drive out and replace the filthy ideas.

Additional Idea: This lesson can also be used for violent thoughts and ideas.

Refining Process

Objective: To help the class members realize that self-evaluation is a vital step in refining ourselves.

Materials Needed: A scale.

Procedure: Display the scale. Explain that to some this is a thing of horror to be avoided at all costs. To others it is a vital aid to help them attain and maintain a healthy weight. Those who view it as a help use it faithfully to measure their weight. If they've lost weight, they are encouraged. If they've gained weight, they reevaluate their exercise and eating and then tighten down on their self-control. This device can be essential to their success.

Explain that as we struggle to perfect ourselves in this life, we have devices that can aid us. These devices for self-evaluation are prayer, fasting, and scriptures. Through these we can find out how the Lord feels we're progressing. We gain insight into areas that need work, as well as receive encouragement for a job well done.

Refining Process

Objective: To gain an understanding that self-evaluation is a key tool in refining ourselves.

Materials Needed: A pail of sand, a sifter, and a tray. Have a few sticks and stones mixed in with the sand.

Procedure: Explain that with clean sand, cement mix, and water, you can make a strong concrete mixture that will set up hard without any cracks or faults in it. If there is debris in the sand, it will eventually result in cracks in the concrete. In order to clean the sand, you will run it through the sifter. Begin to do this. Explain that it can be time-consuming and bothersome but is worth the effort to make the finished product exceptional.

Liken this to our lives. We are like the sand with some debris in it. We have been given this lifetime to refine ourselves and remove that debris. The tools that can assist us are fasting, prayer, and the scriptures. Through using these, we can recognize those things that need attention in our lives. This can be a long and painful process, but the end result will be worth the effort. If we give our Heavenly Father unfit material, we cannot expect him to develop it into something as strong and faultless as he is. However, he has promised that if we are able to offer him ourselves in a refined and worthy state, we can become like him, strong and perfect, without cracks or faults.

Repentance

Objective: To illustrate why repentance is important.

Materials Needed: A doormat.

Procedure: Display the doormat, and point out that it is put in front of the door to provide those who enter the opportunity to wipe the dirt and debris from their feet so that they will not soil the inside of the home.

Explain that Heavenly Father has also placed a door-mat outside his home. It is known as repentance. Repentance enables us to remove the things from our lives that are not clean. Explain further that unless we cleanse our lives of such debris, we will not be allowed into our Father's house.

Repentance

Objective: To show the four Rs of repentance: recognition, regret, relinquishment of sin (including confession), and restitution.

Materials Needed: A hammer, nails, wood putty, and a thick board.

Procedure: Discuss each of the four Rs of repentance with the class.

Explain that the board is like ourselves and the nails are like sins we commit. Take a nail and label it with a name (gossiping, stealing, lying, etc.). Hammer it into the board. Repeat until several nails are in the board.

Express shock at how badly the board looks (recognition). State how much you would like to have the board smooth again and how badly you feel that the nails were put there (regret). Take action to remove the nails. When the nails are removed, tell how determined you are that no more nails be put into your board (relinquishment). Carefully apply wood putty to the nail holes, and allow it to dry while you discuss ways to recompense various sins (restitution).

Discuss what would have happened to the board if any of the steps would have been skipped (restitution could not be accomplished without relinquishing the sin, relinquishment would not have happened without recognition or regret, etc.). Explain that in order to fully repent, all four steps must be taken.

Repentance

Objective: To show that sin can leave marks but that repentance can make us clean.

Materials Needed: One hard-boiled egg, one dish of food coloring, and water.

Procedure: Show the white, hard-boiled egg to the class. Dip the egg into the colored water, and observe what happens. Have the class comment on what happens to the egg as you continue to dip it in the colored water.

Explain that we are like the colored egg. Whenever we lower our standards or our actions to a worldly or physical level, we take on some of the characteristics of that level. We become stained.

Now begin to peel the egg. Discuss how repentance can take the stain of sin away and leave us white and pure.

Repentance

Objective: To depict our opportunity to rise up and be a renewed person through repentance.

Materials Needed: A plastic strawberry basket, four helium-filled balloons on strings, and four medium-sized rocks.

Procedure: Begin this lesson by giving a brief explanation of what repentance is. Be sure to include the four basic steps: (1) regret for the sin, (2) abandonment of the sin, (3) confession, and (4) restitution.

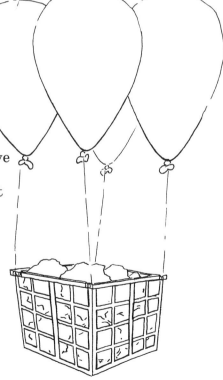

Display the strawberry basket, which is filled with the rocks. Each corner of the strawberry basket should have a balloon tied securely to it.

Liken the stones to sins because they weight us down. If we go through the proper repentance process, we can remove the sins from our lives. Remove the stones one by one. The basket will lighten a little as each stone is removed. Before taking away the last stone, point out that repentance makes it possible for us to rise up and reach our highest potential. Remove the final stone, and the helium balloons will lift the strawberry basket to the ceiling.

Repentance

Objective: To show that sin can be removed.

Materials Needed: Ink, glass of water, bleach, and an eyedropper.

Preparation: This activity may need some prior practice.

Procedure: Show the glass of water, and make observations about its purity. Use the eyedropper to drop ink into the water, one drop at a time. Talk about how the water is getting increasingly impure.

Explain that after we are baptized, we are like the clean, pure water. Sin is like the ink, and it makes our spirits become slightly dirty.

Pour bleach into the water, and explain that repentance is like the bleach. If we sincerely repent and replace our sins with good actions, we can become as clean as we were after baptism.

Resurrection

Objective: To gain a better understanding of the Resurrection.

Materials Needed: An ink pen with an ink cartridge that can be removed.

Procedure: Begin this lesson by comparing the pen and ink cartridge with our body and spirit. When we are born, our spirit enters our body. Place the ink cartridge inside the pen. Explain that we can accomplish many things when our spirits are coupled with our mortal bodies. Draw a simple sketch or picture. When we die, our spirits are removed from our bodies. Take the cartridge out of the pen, and lay the pen down. Explain that the mortal body is left behind and the spirit goes on. The spirit can still do many things, though not as easily. Christ has promised us that someday we will be resurrected, or that our spirits will be reunited with our bodies. Slip the ink cartridge back into the pen. Explain that after our bodies and spirits are reunited, we are promised that they will never be separated again.

Scripture Reference: Alma 11:45.

Scriptures

Objective: To encourage us to draw close to the scriptures.

Materials Needed: Two pie pans, a rock, a sponge, and water.

Procedure: Fill both pie pans with water. In one pan place the rock. In the other pan place the sponge. Ask the group which object they think is absorbing the most water (the sponge). Further illustrate this point by lifting up both the rock and the sponge and gently shaking them. The class members will observe that the sponge contained a large amount of water, while the rock just had a few drops on its surface.

Explain that scripture study can be much the same as this demonstration. We can be like the rock. We can read the scriptures yet never absorb them into our lives. Or we can be like the sponge, not only reading the scriptures but also drawing them into our lives and applying the gospel principles taught within them.

Scriptures

Objective: To show that scriptures are necessary in preaching the gospel. (If desired, this lesson can be used to focus on the Book of Mormon rather than the scriptures in general.)

Materials Needed: Two bells.

Preparation: Take the clapper out of one of the bells, or wrap it to deaden the sound.

Procedure: Show the two bells. Explain that teaching the gospel without using the scriptures is like trying to ring a bell without a clapper. Illustrate this by using the silent or deadened bell.

Explain that when we use the scriptures, the gospel can be preached with a clearness that is not present otherwise. Ring the bell with the normal clapper to illustrate this.

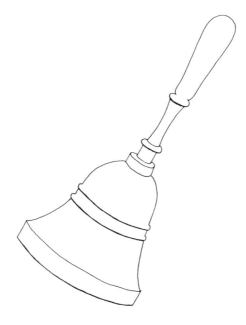

Scriptures

Objective: To encourage us to study and ponder the scriptures.

Preparation: Prepare and serve a well-balanced meal.

Procedure: This activity involves serving your group a meal. As you are placing the food items on the table, point out to the class that you included something from each of the food groups to make sure the meal was nutritious. Also tell them you prepared it carefully so that it would taste good. After everything has been put on the table and the students have had a moment to look at it, tell them that you hoped they enjoyed it and begin removing the dishes. As they begin to question what you're doing, ask them a couple of questions. Ask them if they want to eat it. Ask them if just looking at it will satisfy their hunger or strengthen their bodies.

Have the group go ahead and eat the meal. As you're doing so, make a comparison between this experience and scripture study. Heavenly Father has prepared a spiritual feast for us, with all the things we need. The table is set and all is waiting for us. In order to benefit from this feast, we must actively partake of them. Share your desire that they might not let this feast go to waste.

Sealing Power

Objective: To illustrate what it means to be sealed as a family.

Materials Needed: Two envelopes and two sets of pictures of individual family members. If pictures are unavailable, simply write the names on separate papers.

Procedure: Place a set of family pictures in each envelope. Leave one envelope open; seal the other.

Hold up both envelopes, and explain that the open one represents a family who has not been sealed for eternity in the temple. The closed envelope represents a family that has been sealed. Point out to your group that all families will have problems and trials during earth life. Give a few examples, such as poor health, financial problems, busy schedules, and death. With each example, shake the envelopes. Soon the pictures from the open envelope will start to fall, scattering onto the ground.

This will illustrate that the families that are not sealed will be separated by these earthly problems. However, the families that are sealed for eternity can remain together no matter what trial comes to them, if they live righteously and remain worthy to receive the blessings of being sealed.

Self-Control

Objective: To demonstrate the negative effects of losing our temper.

Materials Needed: Two cans of soup and two pots.

Procedure: Place a can of soup into each pot. Show the group the first pot. Ask them what would happen if you opened the can, poured the soup into the pot, put the pot on the stove, turned it on high, and left it for an hour. It would boil over, burn the soup, and make a terrible mess all over the stove and pot.

Contrast this by taking the second pot and asking what would happen if you put this pot on the stove on low heat and closely monitored it, stirring the soup when necessary. The result would be an edible pot of warm soup, with minimum cleanup.

Compare this to our tempers. If we let them go unchecked, we usually have nothing to show for it, except a huge mess to clean up. On the other hand, if we practice self-control and monitor our emotions and actions, we are more productive, and our self-esteem grows as we feel more capable of handling life's ups and downs.

Scripture Reference: Proverbs 14:29.

Self-Control

Objective: To demonstrate how vital it is that we practice self-control in all areas of our lives.

Materials Needed: A kite, string, and a windy day.

Procedure: Precede this activity with a discussion of self-control. Stress the importance of keeping in check our emotions, desires, and actions. If we give up control and let our feelings determine our actions, we have lost the battle. Success would be nearly impossible.

Take the group outside to fly a kite. After you have it flying steadily, point out that we are much like the kite, and the string we are holding onto is self-control. If we let go of those reins of self-control, the effects on our lives would be disastrous. Let go of the string, and the kite will crash to the ground.

Once again get the kite airborne. As you are flying it, point out the careful direction you must give the kite to keep it from danger, such as trees and power lines. Also point out the constant tension you must apply to keep it just where you want it. Explain that self-control is much the same. We cannot let go of our self-control even for a moment. Also we have to continually monitor and evaluate ourselves to determine if we are in a safe area. Give each person the opportunity to fly the kite.

Spiritual Discernment

Objective: To demonstrate that familiarity with gospel teachings can be an aid in moments of spiritual blindness.

Materials Needed: Blindfolds for every participating member.

Procedure: Seat everyone on the floor in a circle. Tell the class that they are going on a long journey. Ask everyone to remove one shoe and place it in a center pile. Then blindfold everyone in the circle, and mix up the pile of shoes. Instruct each person to find his or her shoe. (Set a time limit.)

Not all class members will find their shoes. Ask those that did find their shoes how they knew they were theirs. Most answers will include the idea of knowing what the students were looking for, such as a broken shoelace, boots, sandals, or the pattern on a sole.

Remind everyone that life is a long journey with moments of spiritual blindness or uncertainty. By knowing gospel principles, we become familiar enough with them that, even during times of doubt, we will still know what we're looking for.

Spiritual Guidance

Objective: To give individuals an experience in following spiritual instruction.

Materials Needed: Chairs, blindfold, and several class members.

Preparation: Set up chairs to make a maze or simply place them in a very disorganized fashion.

Procedure: Choose one person to be "it," and put the blindfold on him. Choose another person to represent spiritual guidance. Tell the person who is it that you are going to send him to mortality and that there will be things that he can run into. Remind him that he can always have spiritual guidance available to him through the Light of Christ, the Holy Ghost, and other means. He must listen carefully to the right voice, because the voices of the world will also be in mortality.

Take time to tell everyone of the rules to this game: no one may touch the person who is "it" at any time, the voices of the world may move around the room but may not physically interfere with the person's spiritual guidance, the person who is "it" may use his hands to keep from falling, and no one may move an obstacle.

Send the voices of the world into the room, and have the person and his spiritual guidance then enter the room. Proceed with the game.

Spirituality

Objective: To understand that developing spirituality is a continual process.

Materials Needed: A pan and water.

Procedure: Bring a small amount of water to boil in a pan. Have the group gather around and watch as it boils. While you're doing this, liken the heat that causes the water to boil to our Heavenly Father. The water represents our spirituality. The steam can be compared to the energy we put forth in our daily challenges, such as resisting temptation, performing service, and fulfilling church callings.

Watch what happens as the water continues to boil. Very soon it will boil away. Explain that to keep the water boiling, we must continually replenish the water supply. In the same respect, we must also replenish our own spiritual supply. This is done through studying scriptures, fasting, praying, and obeying the commandments.

Spirituality

Objective: To demonstrate how being in tune with the Spirit can benefit us.

Materials Needed: A radio.

Procedure: Make sure the dial of the radio is not tuned in to a station. Turn the radio on, and let the group hear the static for a moment. Ask them if they were trying to get some important information what they would do. (Tune in to a nearby station.) Begin to tune the radio. Note that as you draw closer to a station, you get some information, but it's in bits and pieces, and a little fuzzy. Completely tune the radio in. Point out how strong and clear it is.

Liken this to how we must tune into the Spirit. If we draw near to our power source, our Heavenly Father, and tune ourselves in spiritually through scriptures, prayer, and fasting, we can receive the important information that we'll need to successfully run our lives.

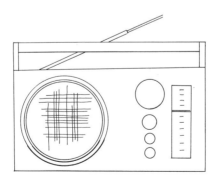

Spirituality

Objective: To show that all parts of the gospel are important.

Materials Needed: A food from each of the four basic food groups: meat, dairy, grain, and vegetable and fruit.

Procedure: Show and name the four food groups. Ask about and discuss the importance of eating from all four groups as opposed to eating from only one food group. Be sure to include the ideas of resulting health, bodily strength, and the ability to overcome disease.

Explain that living the gospel is like eating from the four food groups. There are several things that we should be doing, such as reading scriptures, having regular prayers, and keeping commandments. Discuss that doing as many as we can will help to build our spiritual strength and help us to overcome the evils around us.

Talents

Objective: To illustrate how we can expand our talents.

Materials Needed: A plastic bag of unpopped popcorn kernels and a plastic bag of popped popcorn.

Procedure: Hold up the bag of unpopped popcorn, and ask what it is. Ask if it is edible as it is, and how we can make it edible. (By applying heat to it.) Next hold up the popcorn that has been popped. Explain that when we heat up the kernels, they burst open into a fluffy, white mass.

Point out that our talents are similar to this. They can remain hard, useless kernels within us. Or we can apply heat and energy to them, and they will burst forth enabling others to partake of them. This will benefit others' lives as well as ours.

Teachability

Objective: To show that it is easier to accept the goodness of the gospel when we are warm and teachable.

Materials Needed: Sugar cubes, a glass of very cold water, and a glass of very warm water.

Procedure: Show the two glasses of water, and tell the class that one is filled with very warm water and the other is filled with very cold water. Drop a sugar cube in each one, and briefly stir it. Have the class make observations about which dissolves faster.

Explain that the gospel is like the sugar cubes and that we are like the water. When we are cold, or rebellious, we become unwilling to accept the gospel of Jesus Christ. But if we are warm and teachable, we willingly accept the teachings of the gospel.

Additional Idea: The word *teachable* could be replaced with *humility.*

Temple Work

Objective: To help students more fully realize the purpose of temple work and its relationship to the dead.

Preparation: Be sure that class members understand the plan of eternal progression and that certain parts of that plan must be carried out during mortality, such as baptism, endowment, and sealings.

Procedure: Tell class members that you have a very important promise to receive from them. Have one person ("Johnny") leave the room. Explain that Johnny has been called to leave the room early. Ask each class member if he will try to keep the commandments. Express concern that Johnny will not be able to respond to this request because he had to leave the room early. Tell the class that you will select someone ("Tommy") to answer for Johnny. (Or ask for volunteers.) Ask Tommy, in behalf of Johnny, if he will keep the commandments. Bring Johnny back into the room. Tell the class that Johnny has the opportunity to either accept or reject what Tommy has said on his behalf. Explain to Johnny what question was asked and what Tommy's answer was. Ask Johnny if he accepts the answer.

Explain that this is what is done in the temples for those who have left mortality before they had the chance to accept the gospel. Remind the students that promises are made for the dead by the living but that the dead will have the opportunity to either accept or reject what has been done on their behalf.

Take this opportunity to review the idea of free agency, if you desire.

Temptation

Objective: To show how Satan uses temptations.

Materials Needed: Several brightly colored fishing lures.

Procedure: Show the fishing lures. Comment on how brightly colored and attractive they are. Introduce the purpose of using the lures: the bright colors, metallic shapes, and movements attract the fish. The ultimate purpose of the lure is to get the fish to strike at it or try it. Help the class understand that when the fish strikes, the barbs are set and the fish cannot release itself.

Explain that Satan also uses brightly colored, attractive lures for us to try. Open a discussion about the kinds of lures that Satan might use. Be sure to identify why they would be considered a lure. Close by stating that the best protection that we and fish have is just to leave the lures alone.

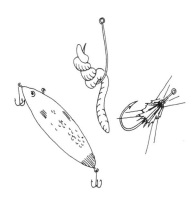

Temptation

Objective: To demonstrate the need to flee from sin.

Materials Needed: Ground pepper, a bowl of water, and a very small amount of liquid dishwashing soap.

Procedure: Approach this object lesson by discussing sin and the necessity of avoiding it as much as possible. Stress that avoiding sin is the best way to avoid most temptations.

Set the bowl in the middle of the table or on the floor where everyone can easily see the water. Generously sprinkle pepper onto the water. Drop a drop of liquid soap into the middle of the water. The pepper will rapidly separate to the sides of the bowl. Tell the students that they must be like the pepper when around sin.

Temptation

Objective: To give insight to Satan's approaches.

Materials Needed: Water, red food coloring, red punch, and cups.

Preparation: Prepare a drink made of red food coloring and water and another of punch.

Procedure: Precede this object lesson with a discussion of Satan's enticements. Explain that he'll try hard to make his traps look appealing and good. However, the only source of true joy and happiness is from our Father in Heaven. Anything else is a counterfeit.

Follow this discussion by serving punch. Instead of punch, use food coloring and water. The class will notice the lack of flavor. Use this opportunity to compare it to Satan's approach. He makes sin so inviting; but once we partake, we realize it's a counterfeit to joy. Heavenly Father offers us the real thing. Conclude by serving the real punch.

Testimony

Objective: To show that a testimony, like a seed, needs nurturing.

Materials Needed: A small plastic cup with potting soil in it, seeds, and a grown plant.

Procedure: Show and discuss the seeds. Be sure to include what the seed could become, what the seed needs to become a beautiful plant (air, soil, water, and light), and what would happen if the seed did not receive these things.

Liken a testimony to the seed. Just like a seed, a testimony needs special care. We can grow a strong testimony if we tend it carefully.

At this point, use the following analogies to lead into a discussion of ideas for growing a strong testimony. Air represents the environment we surround ourselves with (friends, standards, etc.). Water represents the scriptures, which bring living water to our souls. Soil stands for the choices we make, which will determine the kind of nutrition we use. Light is prayer, which brings light to our growing testimonies.

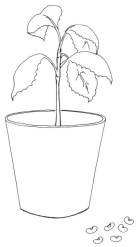

Testimony

Objective: To realize how our testimony can benefit others.

Materials Needed: A reflector.

Procedure: Display the reflector to the group. Explain that it reflects light from another source and enables people who are in the dark to avoid danger and safely find their way. Emphasize that it does not make its own light; it reflects light from another source.

Explain that in a sense, we are reflectors. Our light source is Christ, and we can reflect his love to all people through the testimonies that we live and bear. Through reflecting the love of Christ, we can keep many from the dangers of Satan's traps and help them find their way home to their Heavenly Father.

Testimony

Objective: To show that we must build strong testimonies to survive the pressures of the world.

Materials Needed: A medium to large rock and an inflated balloon.

Procedure: Show the balloon and the rock. Explain that our testimonies can be either like the balloon when they are dependent on another person's testimony or like the rock if we have taken time to firmly establish the truth of the gospel in our souls. Ask what might happen to each of the two kinds of testimonies if pressure were applied.

Demonstrate the principle by putting some kind of pressure on each object (hammer, pin, shoe, etc.). Use the demonstration to lead into or close the lesson.

Testimony

Objective: To illustrate how inspiring our testimonies can be if we bear them with the influence of the Holy Spirit.

Materials Needed: A prism and a flashlight.

Procedure: Display the prism. Tell the group that it is indeed a thing of beauty. However, it can become even more beautiful and intriguing. Take the flashlight, and shine the light through the prism, showing the group how this makes a spectrum. It has become much more dimensional, colorful, and noteworthy by this one simple addition.

Explain that in a sense, our testimonies are like the prism. They can be appreciated as things of beauty. They, too, can become even more meaningful and touching through one simple addition, the presence of the Spirit. If we humble ourselves and prayerfully seek the guidance of the Spirit in bearing our testimonies, they will have the depth that stirs hearts and changes lives.

Testimony

Objective: To illustrate how our testimonies help us.

Materials Needed: An umbrella.

Procedure: Using an umbrella, explain to the group that it can act as protection from rain for us. Though it may be pouring all around us, if we open it up and stand under it, we can stay dry.

Compare this to our testimonies. If we develop and strengthen our testimonies of gospel principles, we can cling to them in times of trouble as we would to an umbrella in a storm.

Threefold Mission of the Church

Objective: To show that the threefold mission of the Church of Jesus Christ keeps the gospel light steady.

Materials Needed: A candle or a picture of a candle.

Procedure: Light the candle, and ask what three things are necessary for the candle to remain lighted (heat, oxygen, and fuel). Discuss what would happen if one of them became unavailable. Be sure to include the idea of flickering or growing dim.

Explain that the mission of the Church is like the candle. In order for it to burn steadily in our lives, we must first implement the threefold mission of the Church (perfect the Saints, preach the gospel, and redeem the dead). Ask what happens when these three ideas are not put to use. Be sure to include the idea that the gospel does not shine as perfectly in our lives.

Alternate Object: Use a three-legged stool, and show how the gospel (the seat) is steadier when balanced on the threefold mission (the legs).

Tools

Objective: To show that tools must be used correctly to be effective.

Materials Needed: A broom and a mop or any other two related tools.

Procedure: Show the broom and the mop to the class. Ask what they are used for. Discuss what would happen if you used the mop to sweep and the broom to wash the floor.

Explain that even though they are the right tools to clean a floor, they must be used correctly, or they will not be effective.

Values

Objective: To show the difference between man's values and God's values.

Materials Needed: Several items that simulate material wealth,* scriptures, individual documents of spiritual significance (birth certificate, baptismal certificate, patriarchal blessing), and a closed box.

Preparation: Place the items of spiritual significance inside the closed box. Prepare the material wealth items.

Procedure: Define the word *value* with the help of the class members. Show the material wealth items to the class. Discuss the value of these items as if they were real and how that value fluctuates. Help the class draw the conclusion that the world's values are constantly changing.

At this point present the closed box, and ask what kind of wealth our Heavenly Father would want us to value. After the discussion, open the box and display the scriptures and other individual documents. State that these items, though in the world, are not of the world, and their value does not fluctuate. Be sure to bring in spiritual treasures that cannot be shown easily, such as standards, faith, honesty, and prayer.

Scripture References: Luke 12:34, Mormon 8:38 – 39.

*Worldly wealth can be simulated by spraying pebbles with gold paint or using fool's gold, large denomination play money, quartz for gems, and pewter or a lead bar sprayed with silver paint.

Word of Wisdom

Objective: To gain an understanding of the purpose of the Word of Wisdom.

Materials Needed: A car owner's manual.

Procedure: Hold up the car owner's manual. Explain that in this manual are instructions from the manufacturer to enable you to take good care of your vehicle. Give some examples from the manual, such as the type of oil to be used and the amount of air pressure in tires. Point out that if these instructions are followed, the vehicle will most likely function properly and have a long driving life.

Liken this manual to the Word of Wisdom. Point out that Heavenly Father has given us a set of instructions for his creation (our bodies); it is the Word of Wisdom. If we follow these instructions, it will help our bodies to be healthy, function properly, and most likely have a long life.

Worldliness

Objective: To show that even though worldly values are attractive, they are only temporary.

Materials Needed: A small bottle of bubble solution with a bubble loop.

Procedure: Take the bubble loop, and dip it into the bubble solution and blow bubbles. Ask the class what they think of the bubbles. Have them describe the bubbles.

Explain that the bubbles are like values the world treasures. They are shiny and fun to make, but they are very temporary. They do not last long and are easily broken. Expand on the positive, long-lasting values that the gospel offers.

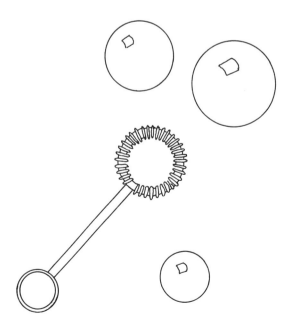

Worldliness

Objective: To demonstrate how worldliness can interfere with our eternal progression.

Materials Needed: A crown made of construction paper, decorated as you like, and three pieces of pastel-colored tissue paper.

Procedure: Place the crown on a bulletin board or similar background. Explain to your group that Heavenly Father has promised all of us the gift of eternal life (represented by the crown), if we will follow the example Christ set for us. By keeping our eyes on this eternal goal, the crown of righteousness, it's much easier to reach our destination.

Explain that sometimes we get caught up in day-to-day living, and our desire for material things begins to grow. We get so involved with what we have or don't have that it begins to cloud the vision of our goal. Place one piece of tissue paper over the crown. Point out that you can still see the crown, but it has lost some of its beauty.

Next point out that we also worry about what other people think of us, so we do things to meet with their approval instead of the Lord's. Place another piece of paper over the crown. Explain that the crown is barely visible. In fact, you're not even sure what it is or if you really want it.

State that another area of difficulty might be wanting to do things generally accepted by society, justifying these things because everyone else is doing them. Put the final piece of paper up.

Explain that if we are not careful, we can allow worldliness to blind us to our eternal goal. Without knowing what a goal is, we cannot achieve it.

Young Women Values

Objective: To show that using the Young Women values can fill lives with eternal values.

Materials Needed: Seven helium-filled balloons (one in each value color) and seven uninflated balloons (also in the value colors).

Preparation: Tie the uninflated balloons to strings. Be sure to put an extra long catch string on the group of helium-filled balloons.

Procedure: Hold up the seven helium-filled balloons in one hand and the seven uninflated balloons in the other. Ask which group of balloons looks the most desirable. Most will pick the helium-filled balloons.

Explain that we are like the balloons. If we do not use the values to fill our lives with eternal purposes, we will be empty (indicate the uninflated balloons) instead of rising to our highest potential. At this point, let the inflated balloons float to the ceiling.

Subject Cross-Reference Guide